Be a Nature Explorer!

Outdoor Activities and Adventures

From the bestselling author of *The Hidden Life of Trees*

PETER WOHLLEBEN

Translated by **Jane Billinghurst**
Illustrated by **Belle Wuthri...**

DAVID SUZUKI INSTITUTE

GREYSTONE KIDS

GREYSTONE BOOKS • VANCOUVER/BERKELEY/LONDON

Greystone Kids / Greystone Books Ltd.
greystonebooks.com

David Suzuki Institute
davidsuzukiinstitute.org

Cataloguing data available from Library and Archives Canada
ISBN 978-1-77164-969-8 (pbk.)
ISBN 978-1-77164-970-4 (epub)

Editing by Jane Billinghurst
Copy editing by Jill Bryant
Proofreading by Alison Strobel
Cover and interior design by Belle Wuthrich

Printed and bound in China on FSC® certified paper at Shenzhen Reliance Printing. The FSC®
label means that materials used for the product have been responsibly sourced.

Greystone Books thanks the Canada Council for the Arts, the British Columbia Arts Council, the
Province of British Columbia through the Book Publishing Tax Credit, and the Government of
Canada for supporting our publishing activities.

Canadä

BRITISH COLUMBIA

BRITISH COLUMBIA
ARTS COUNCIL
An agency of the Province of British Columbia

Canada Council   Conseil des arts
for the Arts   du Canada

FSC
www.fsc.org

MIX
Paper from
responsible sources
FSC® C102842

Greystone Books gratefully acknowledges the xʷməθkʷəy̓əm (Musqueam),
Sḵwx̱wú7mesh (Squamish), and səl̓ílwətaɬ (Tsleil-Waututh) peoples on
whose land our Vancouver head office is located.

While this book may mention specific plants, insects, and so forth, the author and publisher recommend
that readers not touch or consume anything unless they are certain it is safe to do so. Kids, always check
with an adult before touching or consuming anything you are unfamiliar with. Parents and guardians,
please consult with and follow your local park and outdoor regulations, warnings, and restrictions.

I'm So Happy You're Here!

When I was young, I loved to be out in nature and I enjoyed many adventures. For more than thirty years now, I've lived in an old forester's lodge in the Eifel mountains in the far west of Germany. I've seen wonderful animals here and discovered many amazing things about the natural world. Would you, too, like to go out and explore? You can absolutely do that because now you have this guide!

Lots of the animals and plants described in this book might also live near you, and most of the experiments will work all over the world. Your adventures will be even more exciting if you discover plants or animals that I'm not aware of because they don't exist in Germany. Some may look like the ones that live near me, but they've adapted to live near your home. Record these animals and plants in your very own nature notebook. Then you will have two books the one I wrote and the one filled with your own discoveries.

To get started, all you have to do is step outside and set out on your first adventure. Have fun!

—Peter

Contents

What to Take With You

Here are some handy items to bring along to help you discover, explore, and collect. You will certainly already have some of them at home.

If you want to be a serious explorer, keep a notebook and pencil handy at all times. Use these to record where and when you saw or found something interesting.

Plastic containers work well if you would like to examine a find more closely or bring it home with you. Freezer containers come in different sizes. They are light and easy to carry and will protect anything inside from getting damaged in your backpack. It can't hurt to bring along a few plastic bags, as well.

notes

To examine soil more closely, I recommend packing a sieve. It can be an ordinary sieve like the ones you buy at the grocery store. A metal sieve is heavier than a plastic one, but it is not as easily squashed in a backpack.

Bring a cell phone along if you have one so you can take photographs of the things you find. There are also apps you can use to identify plants and animals.

A magnifying glass or magnifying loupe is a must if you are interested in very small animals and objects. You won't be able to see certain features without one. A bug box is a great tool when you want to observe insects. The lens built into the lid allows you to see every detail.

It's best to use binoculars to observe shy animals or animals that are a long way off. For example, you will likely need binoculars if you want to identify a bird at the top of a tree. High-quality binoculars are expensive, but perhaps you can buy a pair secondhand. Or maybe you could put binoculars on your birthday wish list.

It's a good idea to pack everything you would like to take with you into a backpack. That way, you will have your hands free as you explore, and nothing will get lost.

A Few Tips Before You Set Off

This book is for you. Whether you want to browse through the pages at home first or take it with you right away, I hope you will have fun!

There is no special order to the adventures and activities in this book. I suggest you take a look and start with the ones you like best. It is wonderful to explore nature—and the more you learn about animals and plants, the more exciting your adventures will be.

We made this book small so you can review my suggestions quickly when you are outside. It will fit in your backpack, so you can always carry it with you.

Before you leave home, think about what you would like to look for on your next adventure. Then pack what you need before you set off. I've included notes throughout about what items will help you when you are experimenting and exploring.

Make an entry in your notebook right away when you find something interesting. Some discoveries are worth bringing home to paste into a scrapbook or onto sheets of paper in a binder. Include the matching page number from this book when you record your find. This will make it easier for you to organize everything when you get home.

Because you will likely end up with a small scratch or two on your adventures, pack a few adhesive bandages in your backpack. And remember to bring something to drink!

Some outdoor expeditions work only at certain times of the year. Since there are different ideas for spring, summer, fall, and winter, you can use this book to go adventuring all year long.

Now it's time to get started! I have really enjoyed writing this book. I hope you will have lots of fun reading, experimenting, and learning about nature in your part of the world!

activity 1

Checking What's on the Menu

Many birds eat a wide variety of foods, while some only eat certain types of food. What are the birds in your area eating?

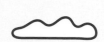

Insect eaters. Lots of songbirds eat insects and bring insects back to their chicks. They might catch flies in midair or snatch caterpillars feeding on plants. Woodpeckers pick ants out of damp wood and drill into trees to reach beetle larvae under the bark.

Seed eaters. Seeds are a high-energy food for birds. You can fill bird feeders with seeds of different sizes to attract a wide variety of birds. And seeds left on plants over winter are important sources of food for birds.

Fruit eaters. Lots of birds help themselves when fruit is available. Berries are popular because they are small and easy to pick, but some birds peck into larger fruit.

Leaf eaters. Many ducks and geese feed on fresh grasses and plants that grow in and around ponds and lakes.

Sugar sippers. A few birds, including hummingbirds and sunbirds, sip sugary nectar from flowers. A small woodpecker called a sapsucker drills shallow holes in a dotted line around tree trunks to get at the sweet sap flowing beneath the bark.

Meat eaters. Many raptors (large birds such as owls, hawks, and eagles that have sharp beaks and claws) hunt small birds, rodents, snakes, fish, and frogs. Birds that live near water, like herons and kingfishers, often eat frogs, too. Robins and blackbirds pull earthworms out of lawns. Crows and vultures perform an important cleanup duty when they eat animals after they have died.

In your notebook, record the feeding habits of birds in your neighborhood. How many of the birds on this list can you find?

Listening to Tree Talk

**Trees talk to one another.
And you can smell their conversations!**

When a bark beetle lands on a tree to bore into its bark, the tree can feel it. The tree tries to get rid of the beetle by pushing a drop of sticky resin out of the hole the beetle is making. The beetle gets trapped and can't get any farther inside the tree.

Because trees react so slowly, they can defend themselves better if they have time to prepare themselves for the beetles' attack. For example, trees can prepare themselves when they are warned by other trees. Trees alert other trees to danger using scent. Every fragrance means something different. Trees share a language based on scent! You can smell it too, especially on hot summer days. If you sniff the air under conifers, you smell a sweet, spicy aroma—the alarm calls of trees.

The most poisonous conifers in the forest are yew trees. Their dark green needles, bark, and the bright red packaging around their seeds are all dangerous.

Trees' needles spread the scent. Pick a few needles and rub them between your fingers. Notice how the smell becomes stronger? Pick needles only from trees that are not poisonous, such as spruce, pine, fir, or Douglas fir.

In spring, you can even use needles from spruce or Douglas fir trees to make a smoothie. Fill a blender with fruit, some greens like spinach or lettuce, a few fresh needles, and a bit of water. Blend well. And there you have it—your tree smoothie!

Discovering Pond Life

It's not easy to see animals underwater. Most are either well camouflaged or hiding so that birds and other animals living in the water don't eat them. Even so, you can still spot them if you look carefully.

Mosquito larvae. It doesn't matter if you don't have a stream or pond where you live. Rain barrels are also a good place to observe water-loving animals. Perhaps you can find one in your neighborhood? Some insects think a rain barrel is a pond. Mosquitoes like to lay their eggs in them. The mosquito larvae eat algae that grow in the barrels.

The larvae eat until they are the size of the full-grown mosquitoes they will soon become. As they grow, they molt a few times, all the while hanging upside down in the water like little commas. A snorkel protruding from their rear end sticks up above the surface so they can get air. Mosquito larvae breathe through their bottoms! If you disturb them, they dive quickly, jerking back and forth.

↰ **Stone flies.** Sit down next to a stream. Lift a stone out of the water and turn it over. Look at the underside. Can you find brown critters with two antennae on their rear ends? These are the larvae of stone flies. It's a good sign if you find them, because they live only in very clean, moving water.

↰ **Caddis flies.** You might spot a small tube moving among the stones on the streambed. This tube belongs to the larva of a caddis fly. To protect themselves from predators, the larvae construct cases out of whatever they can find lying around in the water—grains of sand, bits of leaves, or tiny twigs.

↰ **Frogs' eggs.** Frogs (and toads) lay their eggs in garden ponds, in small pools, and around the edge of lakes—usually in spring. Frogs and toads can lay masses of more than a thousand eggs. The eggs swell up in the water after they are laid. If they swelled up inside the female, they wouldn't all be able to fit.

Tadpoles. Tadpoles hatch from frogs' eggs. Tadpoles look like little balls with tails. Their favorite food is algae. Algae are tiny plants that turn the edges of ponds green, but they also grow in deeper water. In summer, as the tadpoles' tails get shorter, they start to grow legs on the sides of their bodies. As soon as they can walk, masses of tiny frogs and toads climb out of the water onto land.

Little fish. Fish children live dangerous lives because big hungry fish are always chasing them. That's why little fish prefer to swim in shallow water at the edges of ponds, streams, and lakes. Big fish can't follow them there. This makes it easy for you to spot young fish from the bank.

Little fish gather in small groups in the shallows. When lots of them swim together in a group called a school, it makes it more difficult for a big fish to catch them. Which one should it

catch? This one? Or that one over there? As the little fish dart from one spot to another, their bodies flash in the sun, confusing the attacker. It rarely catches one of the small fish, and lots of the little fish grow up to be big fish.

Pond skaters. These insects manage to stay on top of the water, even though they can't swim. As their name suggests, they "skate" over ponds. They are so light they don't sink, and tiny hairs on their feet allow each foot to float on the surface like a little boat. The water supports pond skaters so well, they can even jump up and land back on top of it, which they do when they catch other insects that have fallen into the pond.

The smallest patch of water where you can observe animals is a puddle. For example, rainwater that has collected in a tire track attracts thirsty insects. You can make your own puddle to observe insects closer to home. Place a shallow dish outside. Fill it with water and add a couple of stones to create a safe and convenient drinking spot for bees, flies, and other insects.

Using a Forest Telephone

Woodpeckers use a kind of tree telephone.

> If the wind builds to a storm, you should stay home because sometimes branches break off in stormy weather.

Woodpeckers nest in cavities in tree trunks. Because wood transmits sound well, birds can hear when an animal climbs their tree. Then they look out to see who's coming.

You can discover for yourself what an approaching predator sounds like to the woodpeckers. First find a friend to help. Then look for a long trunk lying by the side of the trail. One of you holds an ear close to the thinner end of the trunk, while the other scratches or taps quietly with a little rock on the wider end. Without the trunk between you, the listener would not hear anything. But thanks to the tree telephone, the listener can tell whether the other person is scratching or tapping.

Windy weather is another good time to hear how well sound travels through a tree trunk. Find a tree that creaks a little when its top sways in the wind. If you hold your ear to the trunk, you will hear the creaking much more clearly.

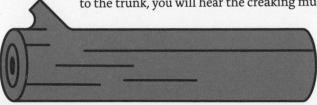

Sampling Algae

You find a green, gray, or orange coating on the exterior walls of many houses. This is often caused by tiny plants called algae— and you can collect these plants.

Algae love moist air and avoid direct sun. That's why you seldom find them on the south side of houses. They grow best on shaded walls that get wet when it rains.

Have you found some? Now all you need is plastic wrap and your notebook. Take a strip of plastic wrap and press it over the algae. When you pull the plastic wrap off, algae will be stuck to the side that was against the wall. Now tape the plastic wrap onto a page in your notebook where you are collecting your discoveries. Underneath, write when and where you found the algae. Can you find algae in a variety of colors?

When it rains, lots of water runs down the trunks of deciduous trees with smooth bark. Algae really enjoy these conditions. You'll sometimes find reddish algae growing there in addition to the usual layer of green.

Calculating the Age of Trees

It's easy to tell the age of small conifers. Just count how many circles of branches a tree has around its trunk.

The branches of spruce, fir, and pine are organized in layers. A Christmas tree is a good example. Every year, the tree grows another circle of branches all at the same height around its trunk. You can calculate the age of conifers, even when they are quite large, because you can see the stubs left on the trunk after dead branches have fallen off. Of course, when they grow really tall, you can no longer see all the way to the top of the trees to count the rings of branches.

Small deciduous trees do not grow rings of branches. Instead, tiny scars form on their branches each year. These scars are what remains of the leaf buds after the leaves have grown. To count the scars, start at the outermost leaf bud on a branch. Each scar marks one year of growth. As you get closer to the trunk, it gets more difficult to find the scars, so you have to estimate the last part.

Spotting Birds

When you are out walking in fields or in the woods, you might find birds you don't often see close to home.

Jays. In fall, jays hide acorns and nuts in the forest floor. Jays are quite large and some are brightly colored. What colors are the jays where you live?

Raptors. Eagles, hawks, and owls are all raptors. These birds have sharp beaks and claws and glide through the sky on outstretched wings. You sometimes see them perched on fenceposts along the roadside.

Perhaps you see flocks of large migratory birds in your part of the world. Swans? Cranes? Add them to your notebook with the dates when you see them migrating. Do they fly by at the same time every year?

Crows. Crows make themselves at home just about everywhere—even in railway stations! Their call, "caw, caw," sounds a bit like their name. If you put out food for a crow, it might become your friend. But you will need to be patient. Crows are highly intelligent—and very wary.

Geese. You might live in a place where huge flocks of geese fill the sky in spring and fall. In spring, they fly north to their breeding grounds. In fall, they fly south to places where there is more food for them in the winter.

Following Slugs and Snails

Slugs and snails are ideal research subjects. You find them almost everywhere: in woods, in parks, in gardens, or around ponds. They can't run away from you—and they don't bite or sting.

Snails carry their home on their back. When they want to hide or sleep, they simply withdraw into their shell.

Snail shells usually spiral to the right and sit on the right side of the snail's body. You can trace the spiral from the inside to the outside with your finger—your finger will move in a clockwise direction like the hands on a clock.

You rarely find a snail with a shell that spirals to the left. Because left-winding shells are so unusual, snails that have them are called "snail kings." Keep your eyes open. Maybe you will find one someday. If you do, celebrate!

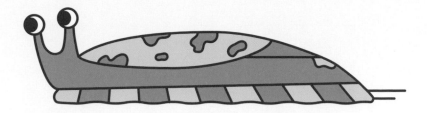

Snail shells are easy to collect. But, of course, only when there's no longer a snail living there. It's not always easy to tell if the snail is still inside. Sometimes snails retreat to the back of their shells and shut themselves off with a kind of lid. This helps them survive hot, dry summers. There's an easy way to check. Hold the shell up to a bright light. Can you see right through it or is there a snail blocking the light?

Slugs are related to snails, but they have no shells. Since you can't collect their shells, how about finding their slime trails instead? Look closely at big old smooth-barked trees in the woods, such as beeches. You'll often find algae growing on the bark, just like algae grows on the walls of houses. Slugs that live near smooth-barked trees love to eat the algae that grows on the trunks. The spot where the slug was feeding will no longer be green.

I explained how to collect algae in Activity 5. You can do the same thing with a slug trail. Find a slug trail through algae and press a strip of plastic wrap onto it. The trail will still be visible when you tape the strip of plastic wrap into the notebook where you are collecting your finds.

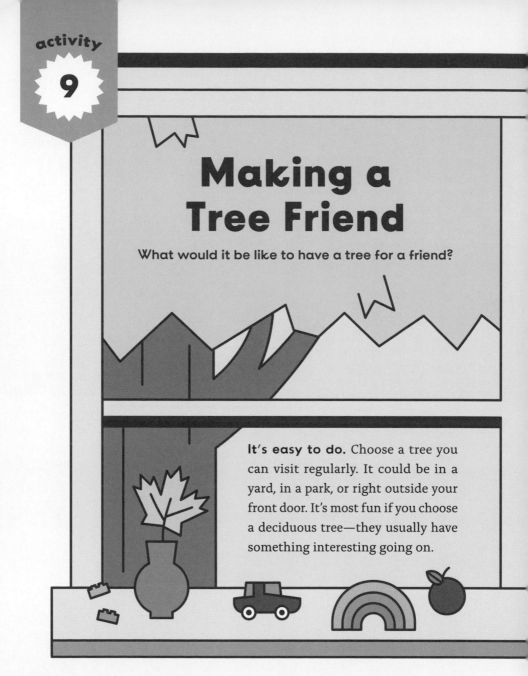

Making a Tree Friend

What would it be like to have a tree for a friend?

It's easy to do. Choose a tree you can visit regularly. It could be in a yard, in a park, or right outside your front door. It's most fun if you choose a deciduous tree—they usually have something interesting going on.

Watch as "your" tree changes through the seasons. Most changes happen slowly. It'll be easier for you to see the changes if you take photographs every so often and compare them later.

Look closely. When do the buds swell in spring? Are the tips of new leaves peeking out from the buds? Does the tree have flowers? Does it produce fruit? Are new twigs gradually growing longer? When do the first leaves turn red or yellow in fall?

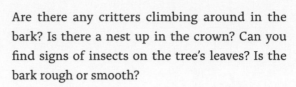

Are there any critters climbing around in the bark? Is there a nest up in the crown? Can you find signs of insects on the tree's leaves? Is the bark rough or smooth?

If your tree needs a drink, you can help. On hot summer days, trees in the city get really thirsty. A single tree drinks up to 130 gallons (500 liters) of water a day—every day! If it hasn't rained for a long time, the tree will be desperate for water and might even die of thirst. But you can help. Fill a watering can and pour the contents around the tree's trunk. One watering probably won't be enough. It's better if you can keep refilling your watering can. Perhaps you can find someone to help you?

Trees need a lot of room underground. They use their roots to find loose soil with plenty of little spaces in it for air and moisture. Roots need air to breathe and moisture to drink.

Young, freshly planted trees are usually the ones that need most help. Their roots don't yet extend far enough to reach water deep in the ground.

You can see where your tree's roots are searching for more room to grow—especially if your tree is an older street tree. You'll often find long cracks in the asphalt that start at the base of the tree. Sometimes you can spot where sections of the sidewalk are being pushed up. The tree's roots are under these raised areas.

A small area of soil is usually left free of asphalt or sidewalk around the base of street trees. Bare soil, however, is not good for trees because it dries out quickly. It would be better if a few flowers or small bushes were growing there. How about scattering a few wildflower seeds? You would not only be helping the tree but also lots of insects, which could then sip nectar from the flowers. It would look beautiful!

Your tree could do you a favor in return. Try this. Sit under a sunshade on a hot summer day. Then sit under your tree. Where is it cooler? Right. It's cooler in the shade of a leafy tree. Your tree is losing a lot of water through its leaves, which cools the air. The tree doesn't like to be overheated, so it's sweating—just like you do when you're too hot.

Finding Signs of Spring

You will find wildflowers in the forest in spring. As long as the trees' branches are bare, enough light reaches the forest floor for wildflowers to grow.

But wildflowers in the forest have to hurry. When the trees grow leaves in May, the forest becomes too dark for the wildflowers to keep growing. They fade away and you don't see them again until after the winter. For the rest of the year, the roots and bulbs survive underground, kept alive by the sugar their leaves made with the help of spring sunshine.

Which fast-growing spring wildflowers can you find? Here are some possibilities.

Wood anemone. These flowers—especially common in beech woods—can be so white, they almost glow. A mass of white wood anemones can look like a sprinkling of snow. In some areas, the flowers of wood anemones are pink. Can you find any? What color are they?

In your notebook, make a list of
the spring wildflowers in your forest.
Which are your favorites?

Columbines. These delicate woodland flowers come in a variety of colors. Columbine flowers in Europe have short spurs. In North America, they have long spurs. The difference is hummingbirds. There are no hummingbirds in Europe. North American columbine flowers evolved long spurs to accommodate the long thin tongues of hummingbirds, which feed on their nectar.

Buttercups. Buttercups are found in moist areas. Their yellow, open flowers look like tiny little suns.

Wood violets. These small plants have blue, purple, white, or yellow flowers with delicate stripes at the center. Can you smell their fragrance?

Yum!

Snacking on Sweet Blossoms

Bees love clover. Clover uses sugar to attract bees because it wants them to visit and pollinate its flowers. The bees enjoy a sip of sugar water as a reward.

You might like this tasty treat, too! All you need to do is pick a single petal from a head of clover and suck on the bottom of it. There's a teeny amount of sugar down there. A hearty sip for a bee is a tiny drop for you.

> You can also try sucking on single lilac flowers in spring. Do you like the taste?

Looking for Tire Tracks

Plants can be a sign that heavy machinery has driven over the soil.

Soil is like a sponge with lots of little holes in it. When big tractors drive over it, their wheels squash the holes. Water can no longer soak into the soil, and puddles form in the tire tracks when it rains. Rushes love to grow in these wet spots. A rush plant looks like a bunch of straight, green wires. When you see a lot of rushes growing in two long, straight rows, you know a heavy vehicle once drove by.

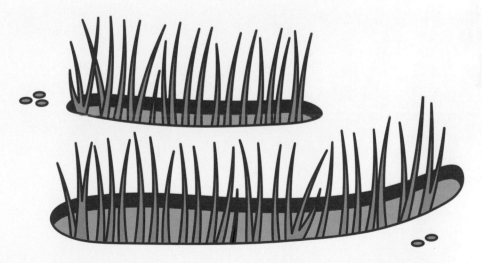

activity 13

Learning About Night Animals

Many animals become active at dusk. Some, like deer, are afraid of people and wait until dark to come out of their hiding places. Others, like bats, aren't afraid. They prefer to be out at night.

Here are some common nighttime animals. Use your notebook to list the animals that make where you live special. How many more can you find that are not mentioned here?

Deer. If you live near fields or the edge of a forest, I'm sure you often see deer. You also have a good chance of seeing them when you are riding in a car or a train. If you look out of the window, you might see deer standing in fields. Even if you can't see them in the dark, you might hear them. Their alarm calls sound a bit like a dog barking: "Woof, woof."

Moths. Moths flutter around streetlights at night. And some have probably ended up in your bedroom by mistake. They fly in through open windows when it's dark outside and

lights are on inside. They are looking for the moon, which they use like a compass so they know which way they are flying. They think lights in the dark are little moons, and they are magically attracted to them.

Bats. Very few birds fly when it's dark, so if you see a smallish something flying late at dusk or at night, it's probably a bat. Bats don't need to be able to see because they orient themselves using the echo of their calls—which are as loud as a jackhammer. We can't hear them (thank goodness!) because our ears are not designed to pick up sounds as high in pitch as bat calls.

Toads. Since they have warty skin that dries out easily and they burn quickly in the sun, toads prefer to move around at night. Unlike frogs, toads sometimes live some distance from water, so they like it best when the ground is still wet after a rain.

Frogs have long legs and jump. Toads have shorter legs and prefer to crawl.

Owls. Owls sometimes nest in street trees, but you are more likely to see them at dusk on the edges of woodlands. You can tell the bird flying by is an owl because when owls beat their wings, they make no noise at all. Silent flight is their secret weapon. Mice can't hear when there's a hungry owl around looking for a snack.

Peeking Underwater

You don't need goggles or a diver's mask to see into a stream or under the smooth surface of a lake.

All you need is a glass bowl, a plastic container, or a large glass. They all work almost as well.

Immerse the container in the water as far as you can without water spilling over the edge. It's best to hold on to the container with both hands.

It's important that your container is completely transparent and the bottom is flat without any patterns or writing on it.

To make sure you don't tip too far forward and end up in the water, have someone hold on to you from behind. This works especially well if you have a belt or a sturdy waistband. The second person can hold on and gently pull back.

Now look through the bottom and sides of your container. What can you see?

Making Chewing Gum

When spruce trees are injured, a sticky liquid flows out of the wound. The tree uses this like glue to quickly close the wound. Over time, the liquid dries out.

You can make chewing gum from dried-out spruce resin. In the forest, look for resin on the bark of large spruce trees. A good drop of resin is transparent and quite large (almost 0.5 inches; about 1 centimeter across). When you touch it, it should feel hard.

> Only use resin from spruce trees and don't look for resin in parks. Parks often grow species that are not local to your area, and their resin might be poisonous.

Pick this hardened drop of resin off the bark and put it in your mouth. At first, do nothing. After a couple of minutes, test it carefully with your teeth to see if it's slowly getting soft enough to chew. But don't start chewing too soon! If you do, the drop will shatter into tiny, bitter pieces.

As you test and chew, spit often. You're allowed to do that in the forest! The resin will gradually lose its bitter taste. If all goes well, after about ten minutes you'll have a pinkish chewing gum. When you don't want to chew it anymore, don't swallow it. Just spit it out!

Counting Tree Rings

Sometimes you find tree trunks lying in piles next to a forest road. If you want to know how old the trees were when they were cut down, there's an easy way to find out—just count the rings.

Here's how it works. Look at the cut surface of the trunk. You will see many thin dark circles, each one larger than the one inside it. These circles mark the outer edges of annual growth rings. Tree rings get their name because the tree grows a new ring with a new layer of wood under its bark every year. That's how trees grow wider and wider each year.

In some trunks, the rings are so far off to one side that the middle one is not in the center of the trunk. That's a sign the tree grew crooked and leaned over to the side on which the rings are widest.

The youngest tree ring is on the outside; the oldest is in the middle. To find out how old the tree was, count the dark lines. Count the dot in the middle, as well. The dot marks the time when the tree was so small and thin it hadn't yet formed any rings.

You can read much more than the tree's age from its rings. Uneven rings mark where a tree's trunk was injured. The younger rings will have gaps at the spot where the damage occurred. The tree tries to close the gap by growing new wood on either side, which sometimes takes many years. If you look closely, you can still see old wounds as thin dark streaks. If fungi managed to get inside, the wood near the wound will be darker or might even have rotted away.

The width of each ring varies from year to year. It all depends on how the tree was doing. If it was thirsty, for example in a dry summer, the ring for that year will be very narrow. In years with a lot of rain, the rings will be wider. This means that even many years later you can get an idea of what the weather was like in the place where the tree was growing.

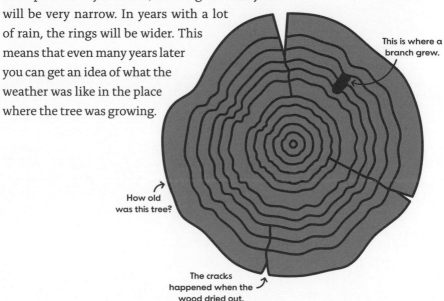

This is where a branch grew.

How old was this tree?

The cracks happened when the wood dried out.

Mapping Plants That Move

In early summer, do forget-me-nots bloom in your garden or in a park near you? Perhaps you've noticed they flower in a different spot every year.

Forget-me-nots move because ants carry their seeds away with them. Ants love—really love—the little nubs attached to the seeds. The ants nibble the nubs off the seeds and eat them, leaving the uneaten seeds all over the garden. New forget-me-nots grow from ant "garbage."

Many different plants use ants to disperse their seeds, including bleeding hearts, hyacinths, trilliums, and violas. Do any of these plants grow where you live? You might find some of them in gardens or parks and others growing wild in the woods.

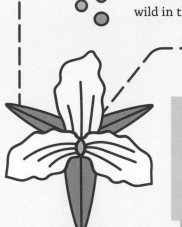

If you have a patch of these flowers near you, why not create a map of where they grow (perhaps by taking photographs or by drawing the map in your notebook)? Then you can check back every year to see if the flowers have moved.

Tracking Animals

Fresh snow makes it easy to see where animals have been. Unfortunately, it doesn't often snow where I live. Luckily, we have mud year round!

The muddy edges of woods and fields are good places to look for animal tracks. Prints left by animal paws and hooves are easier to see in mud than in snow. What might you find if you look closely?

You might well have come across a print like this while you were out walking. Do you know what animal made them?

Wild animal tracks are not as easy to identify. These are the tracks of a wild pig.

Wild pig

In winter, be on the lookout for hare tracks. The photo shows you what the tracks look like when a hare hops along: the hind paws leave a longer print than the forepaws.

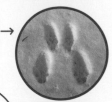

Hare

It can be tough to spot the print from a fox's paw.

If you find tracks in mud that have been hardened by the sun, you can take one home with you. You will need a package of quick-drying plaster powder, an empty yogurt container, and water. Mix the powder with the water in the container until there are no more lumps. You'll find the proportions written on the package.

Fox

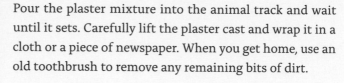

Pour the plaster mixture into the animal track and wait until it sets. Carefully lift the plaster cast and wrap it in a cloth or a piece of newspaper. When you get home, use an old toothbrush to remove any remaining bits of dirt.

Tracks are not the only visible evidence animals leave for you to find. With a little bit of practice, you can find all sorts of clues that animals have been in the neighborhood—and may still be around! Here are some suggestions. How many of these clues can you find where you live?

If you spot little holes in the wood of a dead tree lying on the ground, you can tell which insect larvae used to live inside it. For example, holes made by wood wasps are round and large enough to fit a cotton swab. Long-horned beetles leave oval holes that fit their oval bodies.

Bird parents throw broken eggshells out of their nests to make more room for their chicks after they hatch. Sometimes you find these shells in a yard, in a park, or along a trail. Look on the internet to see if you can find out which birds they belonged to. Draw the eggshell patterns in your notebook and color them in to record your find.

Lots of animals like to eat pine cones, including squirrels, woodpeckers, and mice. Check out any cones you find on the ground. Sometimes you find the centers of the cones with no scales. Other times, all you find is a pile of scales the animal threw away as it nibbled down to the seeds inside the cone.

You might spot a blade of grass in a field or in a yard with foam sticking to it. Don't worry. It isn't spit! A baby spittlebug is hiding in this foamy fortress. (You can see how this bug got its name.) It will grow up to be a froghopper. Froghoppers are related to cicadas, and, yes, as their name suggests, they do hop.

If you walk over a lawn after it has rained, you might notice tiny mounds of soil. These are made by earthworms. When it rains, earthworms come to the surface because they don't want to drown. And they leave these mounds of soil behind.

When you're out walking along the edge of a pond or stream, you might find gnawed or even downed trees. Any animal capable of doing this must have a great deal of strength and razor-sharp teeth.
Beavers have both!

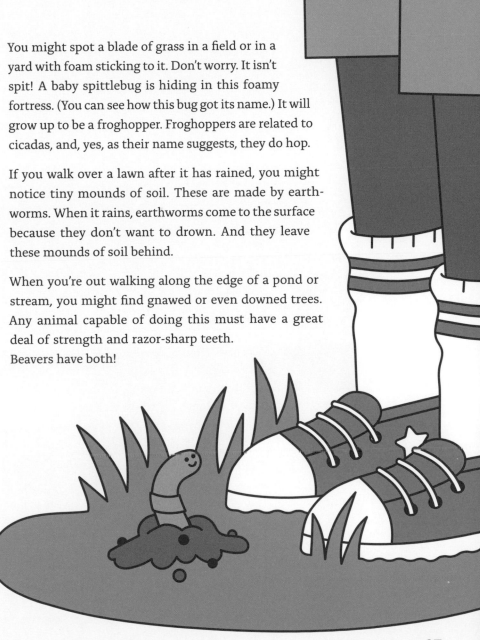

Deciphering Clues

There's always something going on in the forest. Since you can't be watching all the time, it's helpful if you can decipher the clues you find.

Here are some things to look for the next time you go out into the forest.

Tree stump. This is where a tree was cut down. But how was it cut down? Did loggers use a chain saw or a giant harvesting machine? The stump will tell you. If you see a little step to one side, a chain saw was used. If the top of the stump is completely flat, it was cut by a harvesting machine.

> Huge tree-felling vehicles with grappling arms are called harvesters.

Piles of logs at the roadside. These will also tell you how the trees were harvested. If they were harvested by machine, you will find small holes in the bark that go right through to the wood beneath. They are made by the spiked rollers that harvesting machines use to remove branches. If the bark is smooth and the branches have been sawn off, the work was done using a chain saw.

Bark beetles. The needles and bark will tell you whether beetles have attacked conifers. The needles will have turned brown because the attack kills the tree. The bark then falls off or is pecked off by woodpeckers. On the inner surface of the fallen pieces of bark, you'll find closely packed tunnels where the beetle larvae were eating. When conifers are attacked in summer, you'll find lots of green needles lying on the ground under the trees.

Stripped bark. Male deer grow a new pair of antlers every year. Antlers that are actively growing are covered in velvet. When the antlers stop growing, the velvet covering them gets itchy. Deer remove the velvet by rubbing their antlers on small trees, which usually shreds the bark.

Look for stripped bark by the side of deer trails in the forest. If you live in an area with a lot of deer, you might even find this damage closer to home.

Puddle in a tire track. When was the last time a vehicle used this road? If the water in the puddle is murky, a vehicle drove through it not long ago. If the mud has settled and the water is clear, a vehicle hasn't been by for several hours.

Planted trees. Foresters protect buds on freshly planted trees to stop deer from eating them. Sometimes they use white or green plastic tubes about 3 feet (1 meter) tall, which they put over the trunks. You can spot these from a long ways away. Look down into one of these tubes. You'll usually find a deciduous tree inside because deer prefer the taste of deciduous trees to the taste of conifers—and so deciduous trees need better protection.

Earth mounds and hollows. Trees fall over in windstorms. And large conifers fall over especially easily. When they fall, their roots are ripped out of the ground. The trunk is often sawn off and removed, leaving just the roots. The years pass and the roots rot. All that is left is a mound of earth. And behind the mound, a hollow where the roots once grew. It's not easy to find these mounds and hollows in the forest, even though a lot of trees fall.

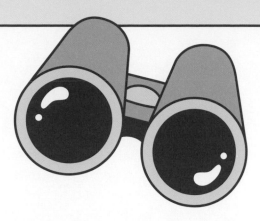

↰ **Rubbing tree.** Do you live in an area where there are wild pigs? Wild pigs love to wallow in mud. That's as important to them as a bath or a shower is to you. The mud helps them get rid of parasites. After they've wallowed, they rub themselves on a nearby tree to remove the mud. The tree ends up looking as though someone has covered it with light brown paint.

Wild pigs have favorite trees they use over and over again. Where I live, these are often spruce. The bark gets rubbed off and the wood underneath is polished so smooth it almost shines. If you look closely, you will often find pig bristles on the bark.

↰ **Barked trees.** Porcupines, snowshoe hares, moose, and bears will eat trees' inner bark. If you find live trees with bark missing, see if you can find any teeth marks or tufts of fur to help you track down the culprit.

activity

20

Locating the Forest Internet

Trees send messages to one another—and not only using scent, as described in Activity 2. Trees also send messages via an underground internet. And you can find this internet if you look for it.

The forest internet is made of fungal threads that join trees to one another like a network of cables. You can see these connecting threads. Push the upper layer of leaves on the forest floor to one side. Where it's nice and moist and the leaves are starting to rot is where the forest internet begins.

The thin white threads you see crisscrossing the forest floor act like internet cables, and trees use them to exchange news. It doesn't matter if you remove a few fungal threads from the ground. You won't break the trees' connection. The messages will simply be redirected around the gap.

It's easy to find these threads if you look in the soil around the base of deciduous trees. Lots of rain runs down the tree trunks—and fungi love moist soil.

Street trees also try to create an internet with fungi. Unfortunately, this doesn't work because the trees are usually too far apart from one another, with streets in between them.

Welcoming Summer

Unlike the spring wildflowers in Activity 10, wildflowers that grow in clearings or along the edges of the woodlands have enough light to grow year-round. Since they are in no rush to bloom, you will find them flowering later in the season.

Foxglove

Foxglove. Foxgloves have large mostly pinkish flowers and grow from 3 to 6 feet (1 to 2 meters) tall. Foxglove is very poisonous, so don't touch!

Fireweed. Fireweed (also called rosebay willow herb) grow stalks as tall as foxgloves and their flowers are a similar color. Fireweed flowers, however, are smaller and grow in distinctive spikes.

Wood sorrel. The leaves look like clover, but the flowers have five petals and range in color from white or yellow to purple or pink. Wood sorrel can cover the ground in forests where old trees are spaced apart, such as the redwood forests of California.

Marsh marigold. These cheery yellow flowers love to grow near streams and in wet places.

White foxglove. Very few foxgloves have white flowers. But one day you will find one!

Clueing In to History

Some forests are not very old and others have a long history. Many of the old forests provided people with food, fuel, and building materials. What clues can you find that tell you what the land was used for or what resources the forest provided?

When I walk in the mountains where I live, I keep an eye out for something very special: places where charcoal was made.

Hundreds of years ago, charcoal burners built charcoal kilns here. Back then, people didn't use charcoal for barbecuing. They used the intense heat generated when charcoal burns to melt glass and to forge iron.

If you pay attention when you're walking here on slopes where deciduous forests once grew—or still grow—you'll find circular patches alongside the trail. These areas are about 15 to 30 feet (5 to 10 meters) wide and flat as a pancake.

Push the top layer of earth to one side with your feet to reveal black soil underneath. If you look closely, you'll see dark chunks everywhere, most no bigger than your fingernail. This is ancient charcoal. You'll know it is charcoal if the dark pieces break apart. If you look closely, you'll even be able to see the annual growth rings in the charred wood. Someone once burned wood here.

← Notch on logged tree

Here's how it worked. First, the charcoal burners dug out a flat round spot in the slope. Then, they cut down a few large trees and cut them into logs, which they split. They made a dense pile of the split logs and covered it with earth and grass roots. Then they lit the pile. Instead of burning, the wood smoldered. After a couple of days, the wood became black and brittle: it had turned into charcoal.

Stone wall
↙

To make sure the fire really was out when it was no longer needed, the charcoal burners poured water over the last glowing embers. That's why the remains of charcoal kilns are usually found close to small streams.

Maybe you'd like to do some research into forests in your area to see if they, or the lands where they now grow, were ever put to any special use. Perhaps you can find marks where big trees were logged? Or stone walls to show where the forest was once a pasture for animals? Who knows what you might discover.

Drumming for Earthworms

Earthworms live in tunnels underground.
If you know what to do and have a little
patience, you can coax them out.

I'll tell you why this works. Earthworms live in tunnels up to 6 feet (2 meters) under the ground. If their tunnels fill with water when it rains, they might drown. So, they quickly wiggle to the surface when they hear the drumming of raindrops on the ground.

You can pretend to be the rain. Take two small sticks and drum for ten minutes on the ground—maybe in a flower bed or on a lawn. You can also push one stick into the ground and drum on it with your fingers. To the earthworms, this sounds like rain.

After a while, the worms come out. They quickly notice the sun is shining and disappear back into their hole because they know it's dangerous for them to be on the surface. Lots of birds—and even foxes—love to eat worms.

Knowing When to Water

Even after it's rained, you don't always know if the rain has soaked very far into the ground.

To find out how much soil got wet, you don't necessarily have to dig. Maybe there's a molehill close by? Simply push some of the soil at the top of the hill to one side. This will allow you to see where the moist soil stops and where the dry soil underneath it begins. If only the tip of the molehill got wet, it's time to water your plants—even if it has just rained.

Predicting Rain

Daisies close their flowers when it's going to rain. By keeping the insides of their flowers dry, they protect their pollen and nectar. This makes daisies a good tool to use if you want to predict the weather.

Daisies also close their flowers before it gets dark. That's how they sleep. So, you can only use the flowers to predict the weather in daytime.

Identifying Deciduous Trees

Deciduous trees are trees that lose their leaves each winter and grow new leaves in spring. Here are some common ones you might find near you.

↞ **Birch.** You will recognize birch trees by their white bark with black flecks. Birches grow all over the place, even in the ruins of old houses or on walls. Look to see if you can find a birch in an odd place like this!

↞ **Oak.** Oak trees have rough bark. You can also identify them by their fruit in fall: acorns in tiny cups.

Maple. Maples have big leaves with between three and nine pointed lobes. The leaves turn beautiful shades of red, yellow, or orange in the fall. You often find them planted in people's yards. The leaf on the Canadian flag is a maple leaf.

Plane. Plane trees and the closely related sycamore trees have green and grayish brown patches on their bark, which make the bark look a bit like the camouflage clothing worn by the military. In really dry summers, these trees shed their outer layer of bark. Their fruits look like spiky balls. They fall off in spring and release their seeds. Plane trees are the most common street trees in cities.

Some trees have red leaves even in summer. These trees have been specially bred in plant nurseries since you don't see red leaves in summer out in nature.

Telling Conifers Apart

Test yourself to see if you can tell the main types of conifers apart. Here's a list of the ones you are most likely to find, either in the forest or planted in people's yards.

Spruce. Spruce trees have short, slightly sharp needles, and long cones that hang down from their branches. Spruce needles are square and easy to roll in your fingers.

Fir. Fir trees have short needles like spruce, but the tips of the needles are soft and the cones stand up on their branches. Fir needles are flat and you can't roll them in your fingers.

Douglas fir. Douglas fir needles grow in all directions around their branches. When they are old, these trees have really thick bark with deep cracks.

Pine. Pine trees have long thin needles that grow in bundles of two to five. The number of needles in a bundle will help you identify which kind of pine you have found.

Cedar. Cedar trees have scaly foliage instead of needles and their bark looks stringy. Cedars can grow very large.

Giant sequoia. Giant sequoia trees have thick, soft, reddish bark. The cones are rounded, about the size of a chicken egg, and stay green for a long time. These trees grow in California, but they have been planted in parks and botanical gardens around the world.

Saying Hello to Spiders

Have you ever looked closely at a spider?
You are certain to find one in your home,
in the basement of a building, or outside in
a garden or park. These are all good
places for your spider observations.

Spiders are
not insects
because
they have
eight legs.

Some spiders spin webs to catch insects. The spider
either sits in the middle of its web or hides in a crack in
a wall or on a small branch. From its hiding spot, it keeps
its legs on its web so it can sense right away when a fly
or other insect lands on it. Then the spider rushes out to
eat what it has caught.

When you find a spider, count its legs. All insects have six
legs. What do you think: Are spiders insects?

Some spiders are really fun to watch. Take jumping spiders.
They are often striped like zebras and hunt flies by jumping
up to catch them. They can't move their eyes like you can,
so when they're hunting, they wave the front of their body
back and forth so they can see their surroundings.

The best way to remove a spider from your room is to get
a glass and a piece of stiff paper. Use one hand to pop the

drinking glass down over the spider. Then with your other hand, carefully slip the paper underneath the glass—you don't want to hurt the spider. The spider is now trapped in the glass. Pick up the paper and glass, carry the spider outside, and gently set it free.

If you are afraid of spiders, you can get over your fear by interacting with them. Try to get close to them often. Why not start with the teeny-weeny ones? Be brave! You'll hardly notice when they crawl on your hand because they are so light. And when you are done, simply blow them off you. The spider won't come to any harm because it immediately spins a thin thread that it uses like a parachute to glide down to the ground. Once you're comfortable with the tiny spiders, see if you can find larger ones. You can look at them and maybe even let them crawl over your hand.

Check with an adult to see if there are any spiders where you live that you definitely should not touch.

Thanks!

Skipping Stones

Have you ever skipped a stone over a pond or lake? To do this, you need the right kind of stone. Here's what you need to know.

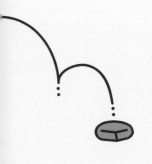

Your stone should be somewhat long and, most importantly, very flat. If it also has rounded edges, you've found the perfect stone. The ideal surface for skipping is a calm lake on a windless day.

Hold the stone between your thumb and forefinger. The trick is to throw it as hard as you can. That's the only way to get the stone moving fast enough.

Bend your wrist back so you can give the stone a slight turn with your forefinger as you release it. That will help the stone skip over the water. Don't throw the stone up in the air. Instead, crouch down and throw your stone as flat as you can over the water.

Count how many times the stone skips before it sinks. Don't give up if you don't succeed right away. Practice helps!

Roasting Beechnuts

You might find beechnuts in beech woodlands in fall. These are the trees' seeds. They look like little nuts.

Collect them, and then peel them and roast them when you get home. Some beechnuts are hollow inside. There's a trick to sorting them. Fill a bowl with beechnuts and pour water over them. The hollow nuts will float to the top and you can easily pick them out. If you use boiling water (get an adult to help you with this) and let the nuts cool, it will be much easier to remove the shells. You'll end up with two piles: a pile of kernels and a pile of shells.

Allow the kernels to dry on a towel for a while. Then roast them at a low temperature in a frying pan to brown them a little. Don't use any oil or butter in the pan. Not only do roasted beechnuts taste delicious, they're also good for you!

You won't find beechnuts every year. The trees produce lots of seeds only every two to three years. Those are the years when it's worth collecting them.

Raw beechnuts are slightly poisonous, but it's okay to take a tiny nibble.

Collecting Bark Rubbings

It's fun and easy to start a tree collection. You don't need much space because your collection won't contain living trees. Instead, it will include bits of trees that you can bring home with you. Let's begin with bark.

Bark is the tree's skin. It protects the tree's sensitive inner wood from drying out. It also helps keep insects and other animals out. Tree bark flakes off just like your skin does. And scars on bark show where a tree has suffered an injury. As a tree ages, its bark forms cracks that look like wrinkles. If you look at bark, you can see what a tree has experienced over its lifetime.

You can make a collection of bark from different trees. The best way to do this is using paper and wax crayons. Press the paper to the bark with one hand. With the other hand, rub the wax crayon lengthwise over the paper. Now you have a colorful impression of the bark on the paper. You can make bark pictures of

different trees this way and store your pictures in a scrapbook or binder. If you also make notes on each bark picture, you will have the start of an extensive tree archive!

If you make a bark rubbing of an older tree, see if you can find a small piece of bark that comes off easily. If so, you can stick this sample to the paper next to your bark rubbing to remind you of the bark's color.

Pressing Leaves

In summer, you can gather green leaves and press them. Colorful fall leaves also look beautiful when pressed.

On a dry day, gather leaves from different trees. When you get home, it's time to dry them. You can buy plant presses to do this. Or you can build a plant press with the help of an adult.

The easiest and cheapest method, however, is to use thick, heavy books. You'll also need a few pages from an old newspaper. But take care. These pages must be from a newspaper and not from a magazine because newspaper will do a better job absorbing the moisture from the leaves. The smooth, colorful pages from a magazine don't work as well. Now you need two sheets from a roll of paper towel and two pieces of cardboard that match the size and shape of the sheets of paper towel.

Take a book and lay one of the pieces of cardboard on it. Lay one sheet of paper towel followed by one sheet of newspaper. Now place the leaves you have gathered on the newspaper, leaving a little space between them. Cover

When you are finished, get your notebook.
Transfer your notes about the tree, its bark, and its leaves
to the pages of your tree collection. If you check on the
internet or in a tree identification book, you will certainly
find out which species of trees you have collected!

them with another sheet of newspaper. Next add the layers in reverse order: first the sheet of paper towel and then the second piece of cardboard. To press the leaves, add thick, heavy books on top. You're all done!

If you want to do everything exactly right, after one day, carefully swap out the layers of newspaper. The leaves will be releasing water, just like a lemon releases juice when it is squeezed.

You can also make pictures with dried flowers. They are particularly lovely if you make them from flowers you have collected yourself.

At this point, all you have to do is wait. After one week at most, the leaves will be dry and flat. Now you can stick them onto a piece of paper in your binder or into your scrapbook using sticky tape or tiny drops of glue. Perhaps the leaves will match up with one of your bark rubbings or a piece of bark you collected in Activity 31. Your tree collection has already grown!

Recognizing Animal Bones

Occasionally, you find large bones in the forest.
They come from animals that died there.

> ⚠️
> If the bones are very old
> and white with moss or
> algae growing on them,
> it's okay to touch them.
> Bones that are not yet
> clean and white are
> from an animal that died
> recently. These are bones
> you should not touch!

There are no graveyards for wild animals. Dead animals are eaten by other animals, leaving nothing but their bones. If you find a skull, you might like to know which animal it came from.

Deer do not have any front teeth on their upper jaw. They eat plants and use their back teeth to grind grass and leaves into mush. The surfaces of these teeth get ground down until they are smooth.

If you find front teeth in the upper jaw of a large skull, the skull might come from a wild pig. Does it also have very long teeth on either side? Wild pigs use these tusks to defend themselves.

Fox skulls are much smaller, and you find them less often. Foxes eat mice and other small animals, so they have jaws like a dog. Their molars are pointed and look like little mountain peaks. Foxes use their sharp teeth to hold on to their prey and bite them to pieces.

Collecting Cones

Collecting cones is fun. You will often find lots of them on the ground under conifers. For example, under pine trees or spruce trees.

Cones protect the trees' seeds from birds and keep them dry. In wet weather, the scales on the cones cling tightly to one another. When the sun comes out, the cones open and the seeds tumble out. Finally, the tree drops its empty cones, and you can collect them.

You'll find the most varied selection of cones in a botanical garden because different species of trees grow there. Ask first to see if it's okay to take cones home with you. In a normal city park or in the forest, you don't need to ask.

There are even deciduous trees that have cones: alders. Alders often grow around ponds or streams because they love water. They have some of the smallest cones you will find: not much larger than your thumbnail.

Most people think you can collect fir cones. But you will hardly ever find one on the ground because the cones of most firs fall apart while they are still attached to the trees' branches.

Building a Sailboat

**If you have a pond or stream near you,
wouldn't it be great to sail a boat on it?
Not one you could sail on, of course,
but a small one you could build.**

You'll find what you need to build your boat in the forest or in a park. A piece of tree bark or slightly rotten wood works best. Rotten wood and bark are easier to work with than fresh wood because they are nice and soft. The best bark comes from an old pine tree. You can pick off a small piece without hurting the tree.

You'll need a pocketknife to carve your boat. You can get one designed for children. The blade has a blunt tip, so you're less likely to cut yourself. Still, it's best to wear a sturdy glove made of cut-resistant material on the hand you're going to use to hold the wood, and have an adult help you. And always cut away from your body, keeping the blade firmly against the wood.

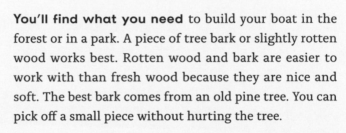

Bark

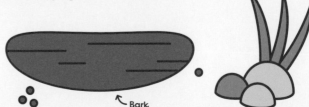

Now you need a small narrow stone with pointed ends. Turn your boat over so that the bottom is facing you. Stick one end of the stone into the middle. It helps if you make a hole first with your knife. Then push the stone deep into the bottom of your boat until it is firmly attached. Because the stone is heavier than wood or bark, it will keep your boat upright when it floats on the water.

Stone ↗

Now turn your boat over. You'll need a small stick for the mast. The stick should be at least as long as the boat and as straight as possible. Sharpen one end with your pocketknife and then stick your mast into the middle of your boat. It should stand straight up.

← Stick

Your boat isn't quite finished yet. You need a sail. You can use fresh leaves from trees or bushes. Just make sure the sail is smaller than the boat, otherwise your boat will be top heavy and will tip over in the water even with the stone to balance it. Now you're ready to sail!

Leaf ↙

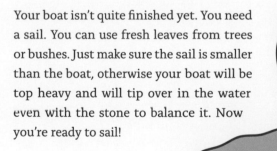

Surprising Your Friends

Do you sometimes walk in the woods with your friends or family after it has rained? This is a good time to play a trick on them.

The leaves of deciduous trees catch raindrops. Look for a tree with a trunk about 4 inches (10 centimeters) wide. The tree should be growing where the people behind you must walk close by it. As you pass the tree, give the trunk a gentle nudge with your foot. The raindrops will fall and everyone who walks under its branches will get sprinkled. Sprinkling your friends with raindrops works best when trees still have leaves on their branches. In winter, it works great with snow!

It's best to play this trick on the others at the end of your walk when you'll soon be inside to warm up.

Your trick has one drawback. You will get wet, too. But it's more fun anyway if everyone gets sprinkled!

Blowing Bubbles

Trees have water pipes running
through their wood. They use them when
they pump water from their roots up to their
crowns and leaves. Since the pipes are hollow,
you can blow air through them.

Take a birch log, preferably one cut for firewood. If you
don't have a birch log at home, check with your friends.
Lots of people have pieces of birch in the firewood they
buy. You can tell it's birch by its white-and-black bark.

Rub a little dishwashing liquid on one end.
Now press your lips together and blow into
the other end. You'll have to blow hard
because the pipes are so narrow that not
much air can get through. But keep trying!
Some air will make it through. The
dishwashing liquid proves this. You'll
see little soap bubbles forming on
the other end of the log.

Decoding Decomposition

Wood is a mix of thin white fibers and dark brown glue holding the fibers together. You usually can't see the two different parts—but keep an eye out for old rotten wood. You'll find it in wet spots such as shaded ground in a forest or under a hedge in a park. In places such as these, rotten wood becomes moist and soft as fungi eat away at it.

↗
Some fungi eat the white fibers and leave the glue. The rotten wood is then dark brown and falls apart in chunks.

Fungi that eat the glue leave the white fibers. The rotten wood is light in color and breaks apart in long strips.

You also find the white fibers in paper, since it's made from wood. Tear a sheet of paper and look at the torn edge. You'll see tiny, short fibers—they come from trees.

When fungi decompose wood, they need to breathe. In winter, you can sometimes see their breath.

For you to see the breath of fungi, it needs to be below freezing at night and slightly above freezing during the day.

On old branches lying on the ground, you might find what look like bunches of white hair. From a long way off, they

Hair ice

look like discarded tissues. These bunches are not made of hair, however, but are the frozen breath of fungi living inside the branch.

Fungi have a lot of moisture in their breath, just like you do. When it freezes at night, the breath turns into ice. But it mustn't be too cold or the branch would freeze completely and then the fungi would stop breathing.

> If you want to test whether what you have found really is hair ice, simply pick it up. The fine hairs will quickly melt, leaving nothing but a few drops of water.

Finding Things That Flutter

In summer, lots of colorful butterflies fly over fields and garden beds. Some moths can be surprisingly colorful, too. I've found a few special ones for you to look out for.

↖ **Brimstone.** If you live in Europe, the first butterfly you see in spring will likely be this one. You will recognize it by its yellow color. It overwintered in its adult form and is off to find food early in the year.

European peacock. The European peacock butterfly has eyes on its wings. They're not real eyes, of course, but to birds, they look like the eyes of a really large animal, so birds leave it alone. The caterpillars are black. The caterpillars' favorite food is stinging nettle, so it's good when people leave roadside edges and some grassy areas in their yards unmown.

Tiger moth. The caterpillars of this moth are called woolly bears. They can be up to 2.5 inches (6 centimeters) long and are covered with furry hairs—like a bear. In North America, the caterpillars sport bands of orange and brown. In Europe, they are brown all over.

The moth that develops from European woolly bears has an unusual coloring. The brown-and-white forewings hide orange-blue rear wings. When a bird tries to eat the moth, it flashes its rear wings, which confuses the bird so much it leaves the moth alone and flies away.

Hummingbird hawk-moth. This moth looks like a small bird that hovers in front of flowers. It can fly long distances—up to 1,800 miles (3,000 kilometers)! There's a related species in Europe known as a bee hawk-moth. The first individuals of the European species usually appear in June and fly up from the south, for example from Italy. Their favorite garden flower is phlox.

Scoping Out Stars

You don't have to travel far to have an adventure! What about spending a summer night on a balcony or in a backyard with a friend? If you get too cold or it begins to rain, you can always go back inside.

In the night, you'll hear sounds more clearly and different animals will be out and about. It's even more exciting if you spend the night not in a tent but just in your sleeping bag. You need one that fits you, and if you put an air mattress or yoga mat underneath, you won't get so cold. Take a water bottle and a flashlight outside with you. The flashlight will come in handy if you need to get up to go to the bathroom in the dark.

Be careful. While sleeping on a balcony or deck, make sure there are no big gaps at the bottom of the railings. You don't want to roll off in the night! Outside on the ground, choose a flat spot to lie on. If you're on a slope, you'll find yourself slipping down it as you sleep.

Playing With Tickly Grasses and Sticky Burs

When you're out walking with your family or friends, it's great fun to tickle someone without them knowing it's you.

This works best in late summer because you need a really long stalk of grass, topped with a flower head. If you're walking behind someone, you can tickle their neck with the soft tip on the end of the stalk.

It's equally fun to throw burs. Burs are seeds covered with tiny hooks. You often find them on plants along the trail. The hooks cling to the fur of passing animals, which carry the seeds far away. The seeds look like little spiky balls, a bit like the outer coverings of sweet chestnuts.

Perhaps you will find some on your next walk. Toss the burs gently onto the jacket of your walking companion and see if they stick. But don't throw them into anyone's hair! Burs are really difficult to remove.

After investigating what made burs stick so well to his dog's fur, a Swiss engineer invented the hook-and-loop fastener now known as Velcro.

Sifting Through the Forest Floor

There are more life-forms in a handful of earth than there are people on Earth! Most of these life-forms are so small you can't see them.

Take a few handfuls of soil from the forest floor, sieve it, and then examine what's in your sieve using a magnifying glass or magnifying loupe. Maybe you will find a few of these animals.

Globular springtail

Sow bugs are related to shrimp and need moist soil. They are gray on top and lighter underneath with lots of legs.

Beetle mites look like small round balls. They are related to spiders.

↖ **Springtails** come in different shapes and colors. The long white ones are the easiest to spot. Springtails bounce around when you breathe on them.

Some leaves on the ground resemble fine webs. Animals on the forest floor have eaten every part except for the veins.

Slugs and snails eat dead plant parts and sometimes even dead animals.

Earthworms are often smaller in the forest than they are in your backyard.

Most **ground beetles** can run very fast. They are large and black and eat other small animals.

Pill bugs look like sow bugs but they are black and roll up into a ball when they feel threatened; that's why some people call them roly-polies.

Dung beetles are large and black and move very slowly. They are on the lookout for the droppings of large animals, which they feed to their larvae.

Centipedes hunt other small animals on the forest floor.

After you're done your research, the animals appreciate being put back down gently on the ground. They will crawl quickly under the leaves once again.

Calling All Ants!

Ants are constantly moving in both directions along their trails. You will find ant trails on paths and in meadows. Once you've found one, you can do a little experiment to discover just how much ants love sugar water.

Stir some sugar into a small amount of water (or use pop or soda). Pour the sugary liquid into a flat plate or a lid. Place the container near an ant trail.

After a few minutes, the first ants will be drinking from it. As they pass along the news that there's something tasty to drink, more and more ants will arrive.

Attending to Business

Sometimes when you are out in the forest you just have to go! To the bathroom, that is.

You can go behind a tree where no one will see you. If you have to attend to serious business, however, it's a good idea to find a trunk lying on the ground. You can use it as a kind of seat. But then you need toilet paper. No worries—the forest offers an alternative: moss! Moss is lovely and soft. Find an old moss-covered stump and remove a chunk of moss. You have your "sheet" of toilet paper. You can also use moss to wipe your hands afterward—you don't even need to remove it from the tree.

Scattering Seeds

Some plants shoot their seeds a considerable distance. One such plant is touch-me-not.

Touch-me-not grows on stream banks or in damp woodlands. The flower looks like a yellow-orange funnel with a hooked end. When it fades, it leaves behind green seedpods. Now things get exciting.

When you touch the tip of a seedpod, it springs open and spreads seeds everywhere. That only works, however, if the seedpod is really ripe. You can test it by touching it—an unripe seedpod doesn't react.

If you have a cell phone with you, try filming the jumping seeds in slow motion. That way you get a better view of how they shoot out of the pod.

Other plants don't need to be touched to release their seeds. Plants like broom and vetch, for example, have seed-pods that dry in the sun and suddenly explode, scattering the seeds every which way.

Touch-me-not is sometimes called jewel-weed.

On a hot summer day, sit next to broom or vetch with dried-out seedpods. You'll hear the pods crackling and snapping around you. Can you see the seeds fly?

Unpacking Buds

In winter, deciduous trees have no green
leaves on their branches. Or maybe they do?

Pick a bud off a twig and carefully open the bud using
your fingernails. Inside you will find a rolled-up leaf
waiting for spring. If you're lucky, you might even be able
to unroll it in one piece. It will be much smaller than a
summer leaf, because leaves grow a lot after they unfurl
in spring.

Some buds contain flowers instead of leaves. Since the
flowers don't have any petals yet, they look like tiny balls.

The casings around the buds are made of brown scales.
Hold up one of these scales to the light. Some light will
shine through. That's important for the tree so it can see
when spring arrives. The tree waits until after winter
when the days get longer. This is the signal that it's
time to wake up and grow new leaves.

Tracking Down Beetles and Bugs

Beetles and bugs are two different groups—or, in scientific terms, "orders"—of insects.

Beetles usually have slightly rounded backs and bugs usually have flat ones. Beetles eat everything from aphids to potato leaves. Most bugs stick their sucking mouthparts into plants and fruits and drink the juice.

Which beetles and bugs can you find outdoors? Here are some tips on where to find them.

Firebugs: On warm, sunny walls and the outside of buildings.

Lady beetles: On plants with aphids on them.

Green stink bugs: On blackberries.

Cicadas: Because cicadas are incredibly loud, the easiest way to find them is by listening to their calls.

Whistling With Grass

All you need is a long broad blade of grass.

Hold the blade taut between the upper and lower knuckles of your thumbs. Now press your mouth to the blade and blow hard. If all goes well, you'll hear a loud, high-pitched whistle.

Don't give up if your grass whistle doesn't work the first time you try. It's important to hold the blade really taut. If it still doesn't work, try using a different blade of grass.

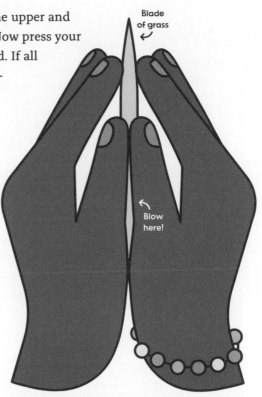

Blade of grass

Blow here!

Sorting Seeds

Tree seeds come in many different shapes and sizes. It's easiest to see which seed belongs to which tree when the seeds are still hanging from the branches.

You can tell how far a seed can travel just by looking at it. Chestnuts, acorns, and beechnuts remain close to the mother tree. They are so heavy, they simply drop to the ground.

← **Many conifers**—and also maples—have a small helicopter-like rotor on their seeds. The rotor turns as the seed falls. When the wind blows, a seed can drift as far as 300 feet (100 meters).

← **The seeds of poplars and willows,** which weigh almost nothing at all, come in fluffy packaging. A strong wind can blow them more than 60 miles (100 kilometers) away. In spring, you find them as balls of cottony fluff along the sides of trails.

Some trees—cherries, for example—rely on animals to transport their seeds. To entice the animals to act as seed carriers, the trees pack their seeds in sweet fruit. The animals eat the fruit and later deposit the seeds somewhere else when they poop.

You can make a horn for your nose using a fresh green maple seed. If you take two seeds, you can make yourself two horns like a white rhinoceros. Pick unripe winged seeds from a low branch on a maple tree. You'll know which seeds are unripe because they will be green. Use your thumbnail to split the thick part. Now you can put two seeds over the bridge of your nose. They are a bit sticky so they will stay on.

Eating Colorful Food

Out in nature, you'll find many colorful fruits, flowers, and leaves you can eat. Before you pop any into your mouth, however, it's really important to have an adult accurately identify the plants. There are also many extremely poisonous plants out there!

GREEN

The most common color in nature is green. And some green things even taste good! In spring, you won't find ripe fruits, but the trees will be growing their first young leaves.

Beech leaves. Why not try young beech leaves? The leaves are really delicate and taste slightly sour.

Plantain leaves. How about ribwort plantain? Not only can you eat the long thin leaves like you would lettuce, you can also chew them a bit and then spread them on mosquito bites or yellow jacket stings to lessen the pain.

The easiest wild edibles to find are red fruits.
Some taste delicious. Others do not taste good
and may even be poisonous.

Wild strawberries. They grow in the forest and also on
slopes by trails where they get some shade. They look like
the strawberries you buy at the store or grow in your garden
except they are much smaller. Wait until they turn dark red.
Then they taste delicious and sweet. You find wild strawberries from June to August. Mock-strawberries look a lot
like wild strawberries. They aren't poisonous, but you notice
the difference right away when you bite into one. They taste
really bitter.

Rowan/mountain ash berries. These orange-colored
berries ripen in fall. They are very bitter and sour. You
shouldn't eat too many or you will get a stomachache. But
they are not as poisonous as was once thought.

Hawthorn berries. The red fruits of hawthorn also ripen
in fall. The berries don't taste of much and have a mealy
texture.

Rose hips. These are the fruit of roses. If you want to try
one, wait until fall when they don't taste as sour. Just make
sure you don't eat the seeds. Rose hips taste best when you
cook them and strain out the skins and seeds to make jelly.

BLUE

It's more difficult to find blue fruits than it is to find red fruits, but some blue fruits taste delicious, as well.

Blueberries. Blueberries ripen in late summer. The berries hang on small bushes with light green leaves. If you eat a lot of them, your tongue turns blue. But don't worry—the color disappears after an hour or so.

Sloes/blackthorn fruits. The fruits of the sloe or blackthorn look like small round plums. That's no surprise as sloes and plums are related. Sloes taste sour and make your tongue feel all furry. They taste a little better after a heavy frost—but really only a little! Like rose hips, sloes are much tastier after they've been made into jelly.

COLORFUL

In summer, the world is colorful and you can find almost any color in nature. Mostly in flowers. Would you like to try a few?

Cornflowers. These are also called bachelor's buttons and often grow in gardens. The blue flowers taste slightly bitter, but it looks really pretty if you pluck a few petals and scatter them over a green salad.

We are just missing something white to try. Either pick a few daisies or dig a little. That's the only way to find the white roots of some plants. Wash the roots thoroughly when you get home to remove all traces of soil and dirt.

Queen Anne's lace roots. The roots of this wild carrot taste almost like regular orange carrots. But there's only a thin layer you can eat—the rest of the root is hard as wood. It's easy to recognize Queen Anne's lace by its flower. Right in the middle of the many tiny white flowers that make up the flower head is a single dark red flower.

Dandelion roots. The white roots taste bittersweet and are good roasted in a frying pan.

Rose petals. Pick off the petals. All rose petals are edible. Some people think they taste of perfume.

Dandelion flowers. Before you eat a dandelion flower, blow on it hard. Sometimes tiny insects live in the dense array of petals—and you certainly don't want to eat them. The leaves are edible, too, but taste quite bitter.

Focusing on Leaves

Insect babies are called larvae. They often look like little worms, and birds love to eat them. To avoid being eaten by birds or beetles, some baby insects live inside leaves on trees. Look to see if you can find any while you are outdoors.

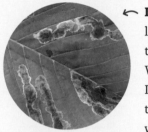

↞ **Leaf miners.** Leaf miner larvae eat tunnels in leaves of various trees. Living inside a leaf keeps them safe from the birds that like to eat them. Where there are tunnels, the leaves turn brown. If you carefully open a leaf at one of these brown tunnels, you will find the larva inside. Later it will turn into a small fly or a moth.

↞ **Beech gall midge.** On some beech leaves, you'll find spikes about 0.2 inches (0.5 centimeters) long. A larva is living inside the leaf, and its saliva makes the beech leaf grow the spikes. The larva falls to the ground along with the leaf in fall. In spring, a small fly called a midge emerges.

Oak gall wasp. If you see a large ball on an oak leaf, you've found the home of the oak gall wasp larva. Like the gall midge, it uses its saliva to force the leaf to grow the ball. Inside, the larva can eat undisturbed.

Pineapple gall adelgid. You find these on spruce trees. The larvae of this adelgid or plant louse don't live inside the tree's needles, but in tufts of needles at the base of new twigs. Here their saliva causes the tree to form a growth that looks like a miniature pineapple. You often find dried-up, brown galls on dead spruce branches—but by that time whatever was living there will be long gone.

Leaf rollers. You can also often find insect larvae in rolled-up green leaves. Look for rolled leaves in summer on deciduous trees and bushes.

52

Acting Smart in Stormy Weather

When it rains, snows, or storms, it can be really unpleasant outdoors. Here are a couple of tricks so you can enjoy being outside whatever the weather.

If you are surprised by rain in the forest, either find a shelter—or stand under a tree. Conifers are the best, especially spruce trees and fir trees. Their needles grow closely together and their branches hang down like a green roof.

You don't have a rain hat? Pick a large leaf from a big-leaf maple, butterbur, greater burdock, or—if you are out in a garden—rhubarb! Turn the leaf upside down and then your hair will stay dry.

Deciduous trees, even in summer when they are full of leaves, won't stop the rain from dripping down for longer than ten minutes. And they drip long after the rain has stopped. That happens because raindrops take their time falling from one leaf to the next until, finally, they land on the ground.

When it snows, it's important to keep your clothing free of snow. If you leave the snow to melt, you will get wet and very cold. Instead, knock the snow off right away and stamp your feet so they stay dry, too.

It's best not to walk through a forest with lots of young trees after it has snowed. Quite a lot of snow will flutter down as you walk by, and some of it will end up down the back of your neck.

If you are out in the snow with other people, you can walk in the footsteps of the person ahead of you. Your boots will stay drier because the snow has been trodden flat. And it's a fun way to play follow-the-leader!

Storms are the only kind of weather where it's important to stay home. In stormy weather, branches break easily from trees, especially if they are rotten. When the wind picks up, whole trees can be blown over.

If you are overtaken by a storm when you are out walking in the mountains, try to walk downhill. The wind is usually not as strong in valleys. Stay away from old trees. It's better to find a patch of forest where the trees are small because small trees rarely blow over.

Acknowledgments

Many children helped me explore, test, build, collect, and discover: Elias, Jonathan, Nele, Mia, Finn, Miko, Nele, Romy, Sophie, Jan, Marit, Henrik, Ludwig, Justus, Juliane, Berenike, Helene, Charlotte, Lasse, Frieda, Paul, and Hanna.

It's thanks to them that this book is so much fun and has turned out so well.

Photo Credits

10 James Gathany, CDC/CC BY 2.5. **11 top** Shutterstock.com/janester64; **middle** Shutterstock.com/Martin Pelanek; **bottom** Shutterstock.com/BranoMolnar. **12 top** iStock.com/emer1940; **bottom** iStock.com/Penny Britt. **13** Shutterstock.com/Jan Miko. **24** U.S. National Park Service, public domain. **25 top** Shutterstock.com/Randy Bjorklund; **middle** Shutterstock.com/Natali art collections; **bottom** Shutterstock.com/Cavan-Images. **35 top** iStock.com/MarinaZg; **top middle** © Valeria Vechterova/Dreamstime.com; **bottom middle** iStock.com/Oleg Zaikin; **bottom** Shutterstock.com/Maximillian cabinet. **38** iStock.com/Birgittas. **39 top** iStock.com/DavorLovincic; **bottom** iStock.com/FRANKHILDEBRAND. **40 top** iStock.com/vicsa; **middle** iStock.com/Carmen Hauser; **bottom** Shutterstock.com/Magnus Binnerstam. **41 top** Shutterstock.com/Zuzana Sommer; **bottom** iStock.com/karlumbriaco. **45 top** iStock.com/timisaak; **bottom** iStock.com/Denzil Lacey. **50 top** Shutterstock.com/KateV28; **bottom** Shutterstock.com/Vaclav Matous. **51 top** William Milliot/Unsplash; **bottom** iStock.com/Anatoly Pavlovich. **52 top** iStock.com/Gerald Corsi; **bottom** Shutterstock.com/Mikolaj Kepa. **53 top** Shutterstock.com/Tim Hancock; **upper middle** iStock.com/Robert Moore; **lower middle** Shutterstock.com/menegue; **bottom** iStock.com/Colin_Hunter. **68** © Jane Billinghurst. **70 top** Shutterstock.com/Nature87; **bottom** Shutterstock.com/Dirk Daniel Mann. **71 top** iStock.com/creativenaturemedia; **bottom** iStock.com/BarbaroSKARAGULMEZ. **74** Shutterstock.com/Lukas Jonaitis. **75 top** Shutterstock.com/Mauro Rodrigues; **middle** iStock.com/Angelika; **bottom** Shutterstock.com/Henrik Larsson. **80 top** iStock.com/JossK; **bottom** Shutterstock.com/Protasov AN. **82 top** iStock.com/AlessandroZocc; **bottom** Shutterstock.com/withGod. **88 top** Shutterstock.com/mayk.75; **bottom** Shutterstock.com/Kuzmalo. **89 top** Shutterstock.com/Heliosphile; **middle**, Rosser1954/public domain; **bottom** Shutterstock.com/Sarah2.

About the Author and Illustrator

Peter Wohlleben studied forestry and worked for a state forest agency in Germany for twenty-three years. Since then, he has devoted himself to protecting forests. He has been a guest on numerous television programs and shares his knowledge through books and presentations, and also through unusual forest walks. In 2016, he founded the Wohlleben Forest Academy, where you can visit him.

Belle Wuthrich is an illustrator and designer specializing in books for young readers. Based in the San Francisco Bay Area, Belle has contributed to dozens of books for kids, a number of which have won awards or been republished internationally.

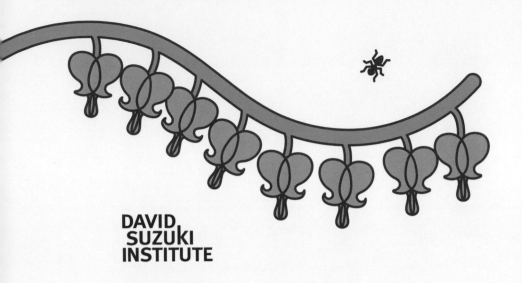

DAVID SUZUKI INSTITUTE

The David Suzuki Institute is a companion organization to the David Suzuki Foundation, with a focus on promoting and publishing on important environmental issues in partnership with Greystone Books.

We invite you to support the activities of the Institute. For more information, please contact us at:

David Suzuki Institute
219 – 2211 West 4th Avenue
Vancouver, BC, Canada V6K 4S2
info@davidsuzukiinstitute.org
604-742-2899
davidsuzukiinstitute.org

Checks can be made payable to The David Suzuki Institute.